ANTIQUES –
EASY MONEY

For the girl who fled the bombs and the boy who fed the lambs

Antiques – Easy Money

(a perfect plan to make money from buying and selling antiques)

By

Ken Ross

Dreams can be achieved, not by dreaming but by learning and by taking action.

CONTENTS:

IT'S EASY

It's easy, making money from buying and selling antiques is as easy as doing the shopping, putting it in the food cupboard, and then getting the food out again to cook a meal. And if you don't believe me then think back to the age before you had a pocket full of money to do the shopping, and the most you'd bought in life had been a handful of sweets or a computer game. Few infants do the weekly shop and cook a family meal every day.

Everything in life is easy once you are aware of the skills needed for accomplishment. Return in your mind to the swimming baths when you were a child and found the art of keeping afloat could not possibly pertain to you. Or remember when you couldn't balance on a bicycle, or when you had no idea how to do algebra at school. Every skill in life is learned, from walking to reading, and from playing the piano to the opening of a can with a release cap. If you can truly understand that life begins in the garden of ignorance and that gradually you accumulate thousands of skills that allow your life to blossom, then it is so easy to welcome a few more skills which will enable you to make thousands of pounds buying and selling antiques.

Already you're probably thirsting for the skills. 'Tell me now that they are contained in this paragraph.' When someone holds the information you need for success a keen desire to obtain it often dries your reservoir of patience, but patience, a trust in maths, and an absolute belief that the result will be what you want it to be are essential factors in your story of success; just like running a marathon, you must be utterly convinced that you are going to finish the course otherwise it is fruitless beginning the journey.

At the start of this journey I shall assume that you have very limited finances and very limited knowledge of antiques buying and selling. My own story starts from absolute poverty and without any knowledge of old items. The interest in obtaining money was inadvertently stirred by my adult children who spoke to me about the costs of rearing a family in these expensive times, and I told them that money is easy to acquire if you have a strong desire to earn it. Of course, seldom do children believe the boring utterances of their parents, and my words fell on ears that refused to listen. Only a few short years ago I decided to show them by example that even a man with no desire for wealth could amass the greatest wealth of his life by following a simple mathematical formula that could be understood by the average child of four years.

But before I tell you this very simple formula you needs to believe that the maths is everything; it is the oil of all businesses, and the antiques industry is no exception.

THE MATHS IS EVERYTHING

Perhaps you have wondered if there are life forms on other planets. I am certain there exists life on other planets, and it is more likely than not that you exist at this moment on another planet reading this very book. My reasoning for saying this is purely mathematical. As there exists in the universe an infinite number of planets, there must logically be an infinite number of possibilities for life to exist on planets other than earth. Equally logical, as an infinite number has no boundaries, there must also be the possibility that you have moved on a few lines in the past seconds to this sentence you are reading now, of course seated in an identical chair and wearing similar clothes to those you are wearing now, and in a distant part of the universe.

This is maths, and maths is a much smarter tool than a telescope, or indeed a hundred year excursion in a spaceship. And if the truth of the above paragraph hasn't sunk in first time, keep re-reading the paragraph until you believe in its validity.

So it is maths that is the basis of the infallible plan to create wealth. And now to the simplest formula that you can imagine: it is so simple that you have probably considered the idea, and even discussed it with family or friends at some time in your life, but never actually done anything with it. I offer you:

1+1+1+1+1+1+1+1+1+1=10

2+2+2+2+2+2+2+2+2+2=20

4+4+4+4+4+4+4+4+4+4=40

8+8+8+8+8+8+8+8+8+8=80

16+16+16+16+16+16+16+16+16+16=160

32+32+32+32+32+32+32+32+32+32=320

64+64+64+64+64+64+64+64+64+64=640

128+128+128+128+128+128+128+128+128+128=1,280

256+256+256+256+256+256+256+256+256+256=2.560

512+512+512+512+512+512+512+512+512+512=5,120

And

1024+1024+1024+1024+1024+1024+1024+1024+024+1024= 10,240

Let me tell you now, I have done it. It is easy. At this moment if you only possess a ten pound note you can with patience and belief turn your ten pound note into over ten thousand pounds and very much more. I will tell you the steps along the way and show you by example just how taking one step after another and working systematically transforms ones into tens, tens into hundreds, and hundreds into thousands. As I have stated. I started with nothing, and over 100,000 multiples the value of my first purchase has passed through my hands. Potentially, in a mere one hundred purchases and sales you can change your tenner into ten grand. Of course, work must be done, and you will need to learn to both identify items and chart their value, but I will show you how.

The first line of the plan deals entirely with ones. If you are blessed and have £100 to begin with you are considerable further on than I was in the beginning. My first purchase was a small vase which I purchased for 50p and sold within a week or two for £8. In the early stages of the plan it frequently occurs that a small value purchase will jump you on a few lines i.e. from line I to line 4, but for the purposes of the plan your rule must be SELL FOR X3. I know the lines in the plan merely double in value, but there will be expenses along the way, and we are not in the business of discovering errors after we have started. The plan must be fool-proof, must come to fruition at all costs, and it will.

So, to recap: what you are going to do is buy antiques and then to sell them at three times your purchase cost. You must reinvest double the money you paid for an item and use any excess for running costs. And I will state here if you are having any doubts about your ability to deal with the tasks to come, forget the doubts, everything in life is easy as I have said, and I will guide you every step of the way. Do not doubt; believe, be patient and trust in the maths.

Before tackling other issues I will just tell you again what you are going to do. You are going to purchase at least ten items which you feel will sell for x3 of the purchased prices. As you sell each item you will reinvest x2 of your capital gain into items more valuable than the original item. Each sale you make will increase your starting bank of 10. Remember, we are on a journey to convert every one of your starting items into treasures worth hundreds of pounds each. Perhaps already you are thinking I am a lunatic. I am not, and neither are you – the plan works even though in the beginning you know you have only maths on your side.

DOES KNOWLEDGE MATTER?

Certainly knowledge matters, but let us assume your knowledge of antiques matches that which I had a few years ago. I wouldn't have recognised a Royal Doulton figurine from six inches, nor could I tell Japanese from Chinese porcelain, or date anything except that which existed in the 1960s when I was a teenager. To begin with scant knowledge is not at all a handicap; an unwillingness to learn is a tremendous handicap and if you think you will get through the plan without a mass of learning then you are wrong. But when you are having fun, and accruing wealth, learning is so very easy because you know it is the power that guides you to greater success.

I previously told you that my first purchase was a small vase picked up at a car boot sale in York on a wet Saturday morning. It may hearten you to know that I travelled to York with the intention of putting my plan for wealth into action. Perhaps I had ten pounds in my pocket, but in my head was the idea that I should buy something which I knew would be worth more money than that I would pay for it. I browsed scores of tables filled with thousands of objects I could not identify. I could not tell anyone the reason why one item may be priced at £20 and another at £2 – it was all junk, all a mystery, but I firmly believed that the small colourful vase was worth 50p and it would make me my first profit.

When I arrived home I looked at pictures of small colourful vases on my computer and discovered that my 50p purchase was indeed a fairly modern Chinese cloisonné vase with very limited value. However, I learned what cloisonné looked like and felt like, and that items could be worth a few pounds or a few thousand pounds, and primarily that millions of cloisonné vases and bowls and other items had been produced in the Far East for hundreds of years, and that pieces of cloisonné and other objects weren't all the same and it may prove expedient to learn a few things about cloisonné.

I had gathered a speck of knowledge that would be useful on my next trip to a car boot sale. And this procedure of going to sales or charity shops was repeated over and over again until many objects could be identified and many approximate values assessed. It is amazing how quickly you discover a similar item to that you made a healthy profit on a few weeks ago, and soon it becomes very easy to turn your £1 and £2 buys into £8-£15 sales. Knowledge empowers you and it is a fairly rapid realisation that the mathematical system of going from 1 to 2 to 4 to 8 etc. is a sure fire method of getting richer. The more knowledge you acquire the more able you are to spot bargains, and the more bargains you find the quicker the process will be of ridding yourself of the first few lines of the plan.

I must admit at this point, when you switch from the £1 and £2 buys to the £5 and £10 buys, you do harbour doubts about your latest purchases. You have ideas that maybe you've wasted money on a worthless object, and as you see them lined up on a shelf in your storeroom you start to doubt that the plan is working. Ah, but then arrive the surprises that fuel you through this period of uncertainty. The antique box you paid a whole £10 for at a charity shop suddenly sells on your internet selling site for £60, and then you find yourself in raptures. It works! I'll soon be a millionaire, you cry. What is more relevant, that profit will go a long way to adding much greater value to your stock, and as a consequence your confidence is greatly boosted.

I say again... patience, maths, and a belief in the plan. The plan has no flaws.

So gather your knowledge from wherever and whenever you are able. Search, find, identify and value everything that attracts your eye. But as your purchases become more expensive do not be tempted to take exorbitant risks: generally buy what you know to be more valuable than the purchase price and only buy very expensive items if you are certain they are of greater value than what you pay for them.

WHERE DO YOU BEGIN?

There are at least seven main sources of finding your bargains and these are charity shops, car boot sales, antique fairs, the internet selling sites, antique centres, antiques shops and auctions. Depending on your location not all these sources may be available to you, and depending on your preferences you may not wish to regularly visit one or two of these places. I can tell you now that because of other interests (i.e. writing books) I am disinclined to spend long hours at auctions waiting for the lots I am interested in to go under the hammer. I much prefer to allow others to do this and give them their small profit when I find an item they have bought cheaply and I recognise as being worth far more than what they will accept for it. But if you find auctions enticing, then by all means visit them often as there are definitely bargains to be had. This too may be said of antique centres and antique shops but my preferences have been with the remaining four sources, however this does not mean that you will not find these places to be good hunting grounds.

In my first year of trading I admit to being a charity shop regular as there are so many in the city of Leeds. They are a good starting point for cheap items, but I have also noticed that in the past couple of years on my odd excursion into one of these establishments that charity shops seem to have got greedy and their prices are often much higher than those you find at a car boot sale. So my advice would be to make frequent visits to all the car boots in your area, especially in the early stage of building your stock value. Two or three years ago I managed to leave most car boot sales with my arms breaking holding the carrier bags containing all the bargains I'd found. The car boots are a wonderful training ground for a career in antiques. Talk to dealers who are generally friendly, ask questions about items and quite often you will learn something interesting. Then as you become more knowledgeable you will learn which car boots offer the best items that suit the stage of the plan you have reached. It may be no longer useful to go to the car boot which has only moderate wares when you have stepped up a level or two. For instance, I used to regularly visit over a dozen car boot sales but in recent times the majority of them have been of no interest to me because the quality of items I am searching for are not present.

To recap, train yourself to be the expert booter who can spot a bargain from twenty paces and as you progress don't waste your time on car boots that offer little or no reward.

The other two markets are the antique fairs and internet antique sites, but be warned, neither are for the complete beginner. Both are money traps that will bite off a beginners hand if you are not very careful and pre-armed with knowledge.

In my early days at the antique fairs I gazed in amazement, not just at the quality of the items displayed there, but at the price tickets attached to the items. Your eyes see fantastically attractive antiques, then your brain recoils at the massive number on the tag. It is like going from the £2 buys to the £10 buys, only far more exaggerated. How dare I spend £50 on this? Is that really worth £80? Visit the antique fairs too early as a buyer and you are in for a bit of a shock. You will be the sardine fed to the bigger fish, and you will end up back on line one of the plan.

So when you first start tackling the fairs go primarily on learning expeditions. That is not to say you won't identify the odd thing that is a bargain, but you must stay clear of more expensive items that you don't know the true value of. If in doubt, don't buy. Do your homework and buy it next time if the dealer is still there and it had really been a bargain. Always remember the rule that you have to sell this item at X3 the purchase price. Treat the antiques fair just as you did the car boots when first you started attending them and found the tables filled with mysteries. Most of all don't jeopardise your progress by losing money on an expensive item which turns out to be worth one fifth of its purchase price. And believe me; the antique dealer can spot a mug from one hundred paces.

Now we are left with our final port of call, the internet selling sites where even the ugliest items look good in well taken photographs. The most obvious problem here is that you can't handle what you are looking at. A second problem is that not all sellers photograph every angle of the item that interests you. A third problem comes with bad description, erroneous description, no description and completely false description, so once again, be warned that until you have reached a very good standard in this business, or you are absolutely certain about the merits of a purchase, leave well alone. This is just for now. As you progress you may find that buying antique from all across the world is your most lucrative source of business. Presently this is where I am, but I have trodden very carefully in reaching this point, and so must you if you wish to reach it and be a success.

BELIEVE IN SMALL FOOTSTEPS

Mountains are climbed not by giant leaps but by gentle tiny steps up a steep slope. Novels are written by composing connected sentences that turn into paragraphs which in turn make chapters, and then chapters eventually make a novel. The best antique dealers are created from a process of knowledge collection: the small steps you take making the effort to identify and to value an object are the very skills which enable the plan to be fruitful. Exercising patience is as crucial to your success as managing your finances.

I believe small steps make solid balls of confidence that enable the professional to go about his business completely undaunted and wholly sure of the path that is being trod. When I told you to start with inexpensive purchases I didn't disclose the reason behind the instruction, but the reason is this: a single successful deal can be done by almost any adult human on the planet, and two successive deals can be done by fewer adult humans. As the number of deals increases the success rate diminishes until you are left with a small minority of humans who are able to make consecutive successful deals. Even buying items to sell for a few pounds each, there will be only a small number of people who can sustain the 100% profit margin on every transaction. I want you to show yourself that you are capable of being one of this small number of people. I want you to be able to claim that you have purchased 100 items and that you have made a profit on every single one of them. When you have done this you can say confidently that you are good at dealing. You know absolutely you are good at dealing. Imagine the strength of feeling that imbues your brain. You not only say to yourself that you have successfully completed the first lines of the plan, you know the plan works and that you can go all the way to the last line and beyond.

The reason people fail is that they believe giant strides work and they lack the patience to put their belief in small steps. Ask a mountaineer or a novelist for their secret method and they will agree with everything I say. Ask winners what makes them exceptional and they will tell you that it is because they know how to repeatedly win and other people only know how to lose. The winner has made a plan to succeed and guarded against failure on every step of the way. This is precisely why confidence building is so essential; when you know your ability is without question, and when you have proved yourself hundreds of times there is not a shred of doubt in your mind you can do it again and again. If you buy a thousand 50p Chinese cloisonné vases and sell them all for £8 each then you certainly believe you can buy a thousand £50 Chinese cloisonné pieces and sell each one at a good profit.

Small continuous steps can take you to the edges of that universe I spoke about earlier. Follow the plan and there can be no such thing as failure.

LEARNING VALUES (no value but to those who want it)

Imagine entering your local supermarket and seeing that every price tag in the store has been removed. You ask an assistant what has happened. The assistant tells you that you should now make a bid if you want an item. You offer £1 for a loaf of bread. The assistant now says she is selling loaves at £3 each. You offer £1.40. She relents and sells you a loaf of bread. The supermarket has become a trading house which will accept offers from customers who are willing to pay prices that will give them their margin of profit. If the assistant is lucky enough to get £3, then fair enough. If your offer of £1 is successful, then fair enough.

Oh yes, you will find antique dealers who put prices on all their items, but all antiques carry only the value that the buyer is willing to pay, and if no buyer is willing to pay the advertised price, then the seller will have to keep the item forever.

So antiques do not have a value. You may find on your travels identical items that can range in asking price from £10 to £100, and I've seen even greater differentials than this. It is true to say that I've seen a Japanese Satsuma vase from the mid-20th Century for less than £10 and an identical vase at an antiques fair in Harrogate for £285. I've seen ornaments in charity shops priced at £60+ and found their twins at car boot sales for £1.

Always have in mind that a seller has turned up at a sale to earn some money. And have in mind too that you have the advantage because presently you are not in the business of earning money just yet; you are interested in increasing the value of your stock. He wants your money, and you have thousands of other items to look at.

The dealer will often say that the object is worth (let's say) £75, and that is because he has paid £30 for the item and he is hoping to make a profit of £45. We shall deal with bargaining later, but for now it is enough to understand that the price on the item is solely that placed on it by the dealer; the ticket could as easily read £34.50 as it could £109.70. I'll say again, an antique has no specific value only that which you place on it.

Only two questions should you apply to an antique once it has been identified and seen to be in saleable condition: firstly, how much do you envisage this selling for, and secondly how much can I buy it for? If the first answer is X3 of the second answer, then buy the item.

WHAT TO BUY

What you buy can in some respects be divided into three categories: personal taste, where you are led, and what is available. The journey which you take from your first purchase to your thousandth purchase is an experience complex, mystical and adventurous enough to be the subject of a full length novel. You can be surprised by what you buy and you don't always buy that which you have set your sights on. But let us begin with personal taste which doubtless over the course of the plan will change as frequently as your underwear.

From day one you are following the plan containing the mathematical formula which will bring you fortune. As I did on my first buying expedition to York car boot sale I set off with preconceptions of what I like and do not like, and it is easy to see retrospectively why I chose the brightly coloured cloisonné vase: it stood out, I find bright colours attractive, and I found it easy to part with 50p for an object so appealing. I could have bought an old box or a dull plate, but I served my personal taste and the consequence of doing so proved enlightening.

I was led to an interest in cloisonné because after researching it for some time I believed foolishly I knew quite a lot about it. I should say here that however much you think you know, the truth is that you have volumes to learn. However, I was led to every car boot table that had a piece of cloisonné that proved cheap enough to buy and in a condition smart enough to offer for sale. My stock became a cloisonné treasure store, with no piece of great value, but all pieces very pretty and up for sale at X3 or more.

I had acted on personal taste, was led to hoarding cloisonné vases, bowls and boxes, and having mugged all the dealers at all the car boots I attended I found that no pieces of cloisonné were still available – I'd bought them all! So the money I'd collected from several sales could either remain in my pocket without purpose, or I needed to show obedience to the plan and spend it on other antiques.

Using the same principal that applied on my very first expedition I found other bargains, or other items that seemed certain to be worth more than I paid for them. And these purchases gave birth to more research, and as a consequence you obtain more knowledge and gather more strings to your bow.

Another wonderful happening is when you sell an object that didn't particularly interest you for X10 what you paid for it. Suddenly your thoughts about cloisonné are diverted to beautiful dreams about brooches or statues or Scandinavian silver and enamel spoons. Your scope widens, you see profit in many things when you once saw it in a limited sphere. Over a period of time your personal taste is both subservient and kowtowing to where you are led, and where you are led is the pathway to what is on offer.

All the while you must rearm yourself with knowledge because it is by recognising what you can identify and value that your rewards are gained.

HOW TO PRICE

If you have followed the plan strictly so far you will have purchased items that potentially are worth X3 what you paid for them. Of course, there will be the odd blunder and I hope the worst has been buying a X2 item, but doubtless among your bargains you will have discovered items that are possibly X5, X10, or even times x20 the purchase cost. Perhaps you have looked on the internet and found a prize object identical to one you have bought and it is for sale at £1,000. I tell you now that for sale prices mean nothing at all: sold prices mean everything.

It doesn't matter what antique you are selling you will find a staggeringly different range of prices for that item. As I have said, antiques have no fixed price; they are sold for whatever the dealer can reasonably get for them. The operative word here is reasonable. If you wish to sell consistently then do not be too expensive or you will sell nothing, and do not be too cheap or you will receive scant reward for all your efforts.

A guide can be previous similar items you have sold. Often I spend as much time researching the value of an object as I do learning about the object itself. It is surprisingly common to find an old object which has no comparison, or at least no comparison you can find. If this happens to you then put the item up for sale at a higher price than you intended. If a potential buyer also can't find a comparison, then he may be willing to buy your item. He can neither think your item is cheap or expensive because he has no information to go on.

But most antiques are similar to other antiques of their type and experienced buyers will know the amount of cash they are prepared to part with to get yours. Try to price competitively without ever considering a deviation from the rules of the plan. Always remember too that if you have priced your item at X3 and several identical items are cheaper than yours, then the cheaper ones will sell and yours will be left the cheapest. No antique has an endless supply: whatever you have, one of these days it will be the only one of its kind up for sale on your selling site.

Pricing gets easier with experience, and one reason why you learn quickly to be careful with your pricing is down to costly errors. Perhaps you would not believe there could be costly errors when you are following a plan that dictates you sell your items at X3 cost, but there are, and here is an example of one which is surprising for it is far from what was expected.

One day on an internet selling site I spied a pair of Japanese Fukagawa vases from the late 19th century for sale at £40. They were extremely attractive vases and I knew there was profit in them so I had no hesitation in buying. They arrived a few days later and I came to the conclusion, that as I could find no identical vases, I'd put them on sale at £480. Within an hour of listing them a customer in Italy had paid the £480. I was over the moon. What a buy!

Several months went by and I was researching other items I'd bought on hitherto unexplored antique sites. When I saw a similar pair of Fukagawa vases to the ones I'd sold I was in for quite a surprise. This pair had sold for £1,460 and they were a couple of inches shorter than my pair. I'd been lax in my research. I'd too hastily invented a price because I found no comparison. And it was this incident that made me realise that as much care should be taken when pricing objects as it is buying objects. The vases brought great reward, but had I been more diligent the reward could have been even greater.

So as you learn to identify you must learn to become accurate with the values you place on items. Imagine how you might feel after selling a small shiny egg only later to discover it was made by Faberge.

WHERE TO SELL

In the beginning, when I was in the process of forming my plan to earn thousands of pounds by buying and selling antiques, the question of where to sell had no definitive answer. I'd scarcely any selling experience and so could only hope that trial and error would provide the best platform. I'd done several car boot sales a couple of decades ago, but the world had moved on since then, and my daughter used an EBay account, but made infrequent use of it. So, I was a bit puzzled, but nevertheless was far from deterred.

The first dozen or so items were listed on EBay, and as I've explained, the cloisonné vase sold for £8. But initially the sales were slow; primarily because I had no reputation as a seller and the items I was selling were low grade, and that is not to say there isn't a market for cheap items.

As purchases were beginning to fill shelves in my stockroom I decided that perhaps car boots were the place to find customers. And hey presto, I began to earn £60 here, £80 there, sometimes even in the region of £100, and the pitches were only taking £10-£15 of my earnings. Always, I'd reinvest the takings on better quality items that were put up for sale at higher prices. But the results were far from what I'd expected.

Yes, the quality of antiques on my stall rose considerably, but the takings remained consistent. It had not occurred to me that people go to car boots in search of a bargain. For every ten people willing to spend £2 there is only one holding out a £20 banknote.

Meanwhile the better antiques were filling my EBay pages, and although sales improved gradually they were not what I desired them to be. Again, I had no idea that seller reputation means a lot to EBay buyers and often thought I was being too greedy with my pricing even though I'd done the research.

The stock improved in quality so the decision was made to do the rounds of antique fairs. Naturally, a table slot at an antiques fair is much more expensive than one at a car boot sale, and I couldn't help thinking I'd needed to sell a few items just to recoup my expenses. And this proved to be the case.

At one antiques fair in West Yorkshire I sat at my stall by the exit door watching people leave after a browse round the stalls. In a period of almost two hours I saw only two couples leaving with carrier bags in their hands, and it became apparent that the majority of visitors were having a trip out and had no intention of buying even a 50p vase. Since this experience my views on antique fair visitors have changed little. And one reason I've been able to build a rapport with many dealers at fairs is because they know I'm a buyer, and not merely a browser.

The profits at antique fairs were little better than those at the car boot sales, that is when expenses are deducted from takings. I've spoken to many dealers since these times and quite often, especially if the weather is grim, I will speak to a dealer who has taken little or nothing in a whole day's trading. Certainly there are times when they have good days, but to me a once a week excursion to uncertainty just wasn't enticing. After months, or even a period of less than two years, I turned my full attention to internet selling.

There may be hundreds of visitors attending one car boot or antique fair on a Saturday or Sunday, but it is true to say that around the world there are millions of customers browsing the pages of EBay every single day. Whatever items grace your stock shelves someone in the world holds an interest in similar items, and I know now from experience that everything you possess will in time sell.

Your experience, or should I say your character, will determine the best method of selling for you, but I have no doubt whatsoever that selling on the internet leaves all other methods of selling poor seconds to me. To be able to list items at any hour of the day, with the certain knowledge that a whole world of interest awaits their viewing through every second of time is a method of selling that can't be criticised. I would strongly recommend that whatever platform you use, also use the internet.

THE INTERNET VERSES THE MARKET PLACE

As I have said, everything sells in time, but the potential buyers for your item will vary in number according to the location of your shop. At English antique fairs you will notice a great deal of Moorcroft and Victorian English porcelain because lots of collectors reside in this country, and the dealers are serving their interests, indeed many dealers serve their interests so the prices remain constant and it is difficult to buy Moorcroft pieces on the cheap. If you set up a business that has lots of competition you will be very fortunate to flourish.

At the same time, if I were to go to an English antique fair with dozens of portraits of French novelists and arrange them attractively on my table, I would be fortunate to sell one. There would scarcely be an attendant visitor willing to pay me for a portrait even supposing he was a great reader of Emile Zola or Guy de Maupassant writings.

Let's change our item to an Indian Bidri vase with beautiful silver patterning adorning its body. Again, there'd be little interest, and it may remain on your table for dozens of trips to the antique fair. I've seen superb items remain for months on dealers' stalls because their customer base is simply not interested in the items: collectors of such items are rare in these islands. The trend of local economy is dead, and today we have a global economy where customers await with pockets full of money in every part of the world.

On the internet you can sell Japanese Kutani to the Japanese; Ming, Kangxi and Yongzheng pieces to the Chinese; Nyphenburg and Furstenburg porcelain to the Germans; David Anderson spoons to the Scandinavians; Bronze Eagles to Americans etc.. The market for every single item is out there in the big wide world. The word houses billions of customers. I have been trading a few short years but I could not tell you how many different countries are the homes to my bargains. I can say with certainty that my biggest markets after the United Kingdom are the United States and China. Hong Kong, France, Germany, Italy, Japan, Belgium, Spain, and the Scandinavian countries aren't too far behind. I've sold to Iceland, India, Hungary, Brazil, Argentina, Malaysia, Nigeria, South Africa, and to every corner of the world. Does this not tell you that at every moment that passes customers are waiting to buy an item from an internet selling site? Yes me, a bloke who decided to pay 50p for a small colourful vase has reached parts where my feet will never tread – and so can you. It's easy.

The reach of EBay is vast, and what is more its platform reaches people who have a desire to own what you have in your possession. I often think of all the people in the world who have been separated from their treasure by time and circumstance. If you were one of these people and you spotted one of your treasures on EBay, then wouldn't you buy it, even at an inflated price?

For me a global market place is greatly superior to a local market place. Follow the plan; take it to every citizen that inhabits the world especially those who are eager to spend their money.

ACHIEVING FIRST GOALS

Your first goals are shown in the first few lines of the plan. Do you remember $1+1+1+1+1+1+1+1+1+1=10$? And do you recall the second and the third lines? Depending on the quantity of the items you have bought, after a few months trading you should be looking at a line which reads something like $26+32+1+6+18+43+18+55+22+30=241$. Perhaps you are on course or miles ahead of schedule? All the while you should be concentrating on raising the numbers by reinvesting the profits from your sales.

I should add here that you must also guard against despondency. If you have been dealing in pounds and you are looking at a mere £241 after a month or two, then you may believe this is not worth your effort. Well I tell you now that you are doing fantastically well. Had you set off with £10s you would now have stock valued at £2,410 – what an achievement, and just think of what is to come in the future.

Believe in the plan and know that with each sale your stock value is building. Remember to always reinvest X2 the purchase price of the item you have sold. Buy better items, more valuable items that will attract new customers. Already the customers you have served will be looking on your site to see what new treasures you have for sale.

As with all things, the first steps are more difficult because you have not fully built up trust in the idea of your long term objectives. The confidence which will build is still in its infancy. But I can't emphasise enough the importance of keeping going and remaining steadfast in the belief that this plan will work: it does work and it will lead you as far as you wish to go.

Another thought to consider is the journey from the complete ignoramus stage to the knowledge you have now acquired relating to antiques. You will have successfully identified and valued dozens of items that once were nothing but old items on a dealer's table. There is great satisfaction to be had when you ponder the course you have taken. Tell yourself that you have learned so much, and there is so much more to learn, and every detail I discover will assist me on my pathway to riches.

SPECIALIZE ON PARTICULARS

Sooner or later in your pursuit of expertise you'll approach the topic of specialization. In most careers people are directed to specialize, but I've never believed in this philosophy, and will never in the future believe it is the wisest action. Specialization is a narrowing of interest and speaks to me as a process of gazing into a single hole. I would advise you to keep your options open in all areas of antique trading; after all you are acquiring knowledge of antiques in order to amass wealth, and not with the intention of lecturing on a specific type of antique ware to a crowd of students at a university.

Furthermore, I see specialization as a device that closes the door to all non-interested parties. The dealer I've seen on scores of occasions at antiques fairs with his stand brimming with Moorcroft vases is of absolutely no interest to the vast majority of the hundreds of people who enter the halls. Had I progressed with my initial fascination in cloisonné perhaps I would have gained a small but devoted following of customers, but I would have closed my eyes to the millions who think cloisonné is undesirable.

Oh yes, it is wise to gain specialist knowledge, but collect specialist knowledge in as many areas of antiques that your brain can carry. The antiques markets don't offer what you hope it will offer you at any particular moment in time. One week you may find much that you are interested in, and this week can be followed by weeks of sparsity. You must seize whatever bargains are about, and to recognise a variety of bargains you necessarily must possess knowledge that covers many objects originating from many different parts of the world.

Remember that you are in this business to make money, and quite often you are led to where the prospect of money lies. You may attend a fair with the intention of scrutinizing every piece of French porcelain you can find, but the dealers have no French porcelain, and all you discover is a bargain stall where the proprietors are retiring and selling off their collections of antique jewellery. You very quickly need to become a quick-fire expert in antique jewellery. If you have a smartphone get on the internet and rapidly determine the approximate value of what the retiring dealers are selling. Bite their arms off if necessary; don't lose out on bargains if you recognise them as such, and most of all don't be afraid to buy items which you have not previously purchased. What you will learn about them will hold you in good stead for future bargain hunts.

At least once a month you find yourself getting immersed in products you have hitherto avoided or not had contact with, but each time you do your pool of knowledge expands and the job of hunting becomes easier. Knowledge is all-powerful and it makes the task of progressing with the plan so much easier too. You will leave the specialist trailing in your wake as your carrier bags fill with bargains and he wanders on empty handed.

Having said all this I am minded to say that there is a difference between specialist knowledge and specialist selling. I am very much in favour of specialist knowledge, and the more antiques you can learn deep knowledge about the better. What I argue against is the idea that you should confine yourself to sales in one particular division, for example, English studio ceramics or Indian brass.

Too give you a clear idea of what I mean it is true to say that out of the first 1000 items I sold I'd say there were at least 990 different ones. A little bit of knowledge gained from each one goes a long way.

DISCARD THE CHEAP, RAISE THE STAKES

The day will arrive when you are wandering about searching for bargains and you notice one of those first cheap items that you happily sold for a tenner. A few more strides and you will notice another cheap item you sold for a similar amount. Of course, the temptation is to dig in your pocket to find a couple of coins and buy both items. But you don't.

You have progressed from line one of the plan, and perhaps lines two and three as well. You smile and continue on your way. You are looking for more expensive items to spend your profits on because now you are looking to make sales that will bring in more than a single figure of profit.

So, discard the cheap and do not replace them when you can afford to buy better quality items which may have the same x3 sales prices: you are now looking at profit in notes rather than profit in coins.

It is at about this time that you begin to outgrow the majority of car boot sales and you start to increase your visits to the antique fairs. And just as you got moments of excitement when you sold those cheap items for x3 their purchase price, you will get increased excitement when you start to sell your £5-£20 items for £15-£60+. What is more your certainty in the plan hardens and your confidence in being a good antiques dealer begins to soar. You look back at your history and see that everything you have done has been rewarding, in financial terms (if only in stock at present) and in terms of the growing knowledge that sits in your brain.

Of course, initially raising the stakes makes you question your decision about whether to buy or not to a greater degree than if you are spend a couple of pounds. There is a tendency to make the odd error and find that £15 bowl you bought last Sunday is only really worth about £30. But stick to the plan and put it up for sale at £45 – if someone offers you £30, then take it, if not, it can remain on sale for a year or two. It will in time sell.

Depending on how you are progressing and the amount of cash you have to play with, never be afraid to dip your feet in a few rows of the plan ahead. If on your travels you see an item that you are sure has value much greater than its price tag, then make a bid for it. Again remember the x3 rule. Every time you extend yourself beyond your present comfort zone you are taking a step closer to a new comfort zone. I recall the time I made my first £100 purchase and thought I'd gone round the bend, but when the plate sold for £300 my opinion was drastically changed.

Raising the stakes also means researching items which you have not possessed previously. But you have learned how to research by exploring internet selling sites and sales results on auction sites, and it is the same process by which you learn to value better items. At all times do your homework, at all times make the correct steps and stick to the mathematical formula in the plan. It is working, you will be viewing the first few lines as history and you will be eagerly anticipating the joy you will feel when you're approaching line 10.

THE HUNT

The old black & white World War II films shown on early television more often than not showed a scene from a prisoner of war camp where the searchlight swoops over the ground between the huts and the wired perimeter fence: this powerful beam darts to and fro as the viewer trembles in excited anticipation of what is about to happen; then, in the flash of an eye the light captures the silhouette of a potential escapee and the rattle of gunfire commences. Wow! And this scene is remarkably like the hunt if taken from the perspective of the searchlight director.

The hunt begins when you walk into the hall at the antiques fair and your mouth drools over the hundreds of tables assembled there. You must set your brain to action, raise from every connection within this precious organ all the antique knowledge you possess: you are on the lookout and you must not miss a single bargain.

I tend to walk very slowly staying in the centre of each aisle and casting my gaze from side to side. Perhaps in the beginning I remained closer to the tables but as you become more experienced you are able to spot an object of interest from a greater distance.

Steadily, steadily I go sweeping my eyes up and down, from side to side on each surface, calculating qualities and values, occasionally deviating to scan a price tag or say to a dealer,

'How much you got on this?' Leave no surface unseen; view above the tables, below the tables, and at their sides. You never know where a bargain is hidden.

If you get chance to pass small talk with a dealer, then do so – you are building relationships for future purchases, and it is useful to let the dealer know that you too are in the business of antiques; this tells them that you are a buyer and not simply here for a bacon sandwich from the café. Another trick is to have a carrier with several other carriers inside it bulking its volume; this too tells a dealer you have money to spend, and as far as the dealer knows you have already spent some. It is easy for an experience dealer to differentiate between serious buyers and visitors who waste their time.

I continue up and down the aisles, smiling occasionally, saying 'Good morning', occasionally too complimenting a dealer on the appearance or an item on their table. But my eyes seldom shift from the goods on display; I am here to pounce when the item of interest comes into view.

Patience, have great patience: never be desperate and buy something you later regret buying, never consider taking risks that possibly fall into the category of lost money, and never ever allow a dealer to sell you an item – you are in charge and you are going to buy the item if you want it!

I wander on, carefully restocking my brain with images of every antique I've sold and every antique I've researched for value; you must be aware that you are searching for thousands of items that are filed in your head under the banner of 'profit makers'.

I'll deal later with what happens when the focus becomes sharp and the treasure has been highlighted, but for now I continue the journey up and down the aisles. View every aisle, every nook and cranny where a dealer stands with his wares, And when all aisles have been scanned I repeat my journey in the opposite direction, perhaps going slightly quicker now, but I'm seeing things from the reverse angle and I may pick up something that has previously eluded me. It would be a travesty to leave the antiques fair and not noticed a treasure.

To recap, walk slowly and keep your knowledge conscious in your head, be seen and noticed and view tables from more than one angle.

TRADING PRACTISES AND HONESTY

No-one likes a slime-ball, no-one likes deceivers or those who are dishonest, and if you are to make a reputation in this business, as in all businesses you need to conduct yourself at all times in a decent manner. You must be fair, never cheat, and never sell goods described as being something which you know they are not. You must be willing to apologise for your mistakes and show grace to those whose genuine mistakes have affected you. Each trader builds a reputation based on the experiences of his customers, and if your customers do not find you fair and trustworthy they will soon let others know you are a fraud.

This is not to say you must be weak, a dealer to be trampled on, or a buyer to be mugged. Far from it, but there are distinct differences between using clever psychology to get the best deal you can or trying to convince a buyer that a certain piece would be an asset to their collection than uttering lies and speaking dishonestly.

I have come across dealers who frankly make me sick because they knowingly attempt to con customers. The rule is avoid them, and certainly never be tempted by their wares. There are rude dealers, ignorant ones too, but thankfully these are a minority because most people in the antique business are genuine and friendly. It is important at all times to be an amiable honest person who fits in with the decency of the trade. The more you are liked and respected by others, the more others with like and respect you.

On exceptional occasions you may be roused to the fringes of fury by a dealer or a buyer, but always bit your lip, put the experience behind you and smile with the sure knowledge that a hundred smooth transactions lie ahead and you are not going to be side-tracked by a single arsehole.

DEALERS MARGINS, ATTITUDES AND FLEXIBILITY

One of the first things that struck me when starting to visit antique fairs was the repeated line from dealers that 'I'm only making a couple of pounds on that'. I very quickly realised that this is the most untrue line spoken in the business. Simply ask yourself if you would sit all day at an antiques fair after perhaps travelling 50 miles and setting off in the snow at six in the morning with your hard found treasures only to make £2 on each of the items you sell, and believe me you won't be selling more than a dozen of them, or twenty if you are exceedingly fortunate.

Ha! Ha! Ha! £40 maximum takings when your stall may have cost as much as £100 for a six foot table at a posh fair in Harrogate. I suppose it is part of the humility, part of the charade that you tell your customers that you are only making two pounds profit on your £50 vase, but only a fool will believe you. When I factor into my plan a X3 margin I am much closer to the truth than the repeaters of the £2 phrase.

So never believe what is spoken about margins, and keep your own margins to yourself; it is nobody's business but your own. The margins a dealer creates is a reflection of his skills as a buyer, and if he is a clever dealer, and very good at his job (as you are) then his margins will be similar to your margins. Understanding this is the key to understanding flexibility of prices. For if a dealer has an item for sale at

£100, it is very likely that he has paid £1-£60 for it, and the most accomplished dealer will have paid closer to the £1 than the £60. So flexibility of prices is something you must always be aware of when you are going in for the kill and attempting to strike a deal.

And this brings me nicely on to attitudes. Dealers who recognise you as a fellow dealer know your attitudes have been sculpted by the experience of trading; they know where you are coming from, know what you are attempting to do when you are trying to buy or trying to sell. The attitudes of the unpleasant dealers, or those who remain aloof and have a tendency to look down on their customers, will be quite different. Some snooty dealer will recoil in disgust when you make a bid on one of their offerings. Do not take a leaf out of their tiny minded book. Never insult a customer who has offered money for an item. Politely suggest that the offer is too low but you should be willing to consider higher offers. The dealer who rebuffs you instantly is a dealer to avoid unless one of his items is so lowly priced that you will pull his arm off.

BEWARE OF FAKES AND DEALERS TRICKS

We shall first deal with tricks of the trade, of which I've experience one or two but certainly not all of them. Bad practises occur in all trades and unfortunately the antique trade is no exception. Earlier I advised you to be honest because I wish all antiques dealers were renowned for their honesty, but they are not.

A few years ago I came across a woman dealer at a small antiques fair where I had not previously visited. Her wares weren't valuable but I was in the early stages of buying and thought one or two of her pieces showed promise. I picked up a figurine and out of my eye corner noticed I'd grabbed her attention, though she remained perhaps six feet away. I expected her to say, 'Can I help you?' She didn't.

I examined the figurine; saw the price tag read £12. Without purposely doing so I ran my thumb across the price label and felt a deep crevasse beneath it. What a devious cow, I thought. But that was not the end of the matter. I saw another piece of interest on her table priced at £25 with a huge label on its base. Lo and behold! Another broken item! On closer inspection I found a third item with a sticker on a figurine's neck – the head had been re-glued! I walked off.

The above is an extreme example of an unscrupulous dealer but the lesson should be learned that it is absolutely essential to examine every minute part of an item you are intending to buy, even if that means removing the price tag after asking the dealer if that is permissible, and if it isn't permissible then don't buy it.

Two other things to watch for are the dreaded glue, which is quite commonly found if you look closely, and the dreaded paint jobs which attempt to either disguise damage or are efforts to make the piece more presentable. You must have eyes like microscopes, and believe me they are needed or you are sure to fall victim to one of these practises. But you should always bear in mind that the seller doesn't always know of the attempted amateur restoration; some areas are so tiny that they are very easily overlooked on inspection.

Some items too are restored, but here I must admit that some restorers are so expert at their trade that I am unable to tell that there is restoration. But if a genuine dealer knows the item is restored he will tell you, and you should pass this information on if you sell the piece.

Now I shall tackle fakes, and it is true that experts need other experts in order to determine if good fakes are fakes. Worldwide, there surely must be as many fakes are there are genuine pieces, and I have no doubt in saying that in the Chinese porcelain market there are many more fakes than genuine pieces.

So what do you do? How do you go about distinguishing a fake from a genuine item? I've got to admit that this is one of my most recurring problems because the bulk of my trade is dealing in Chinese and Japanese items, and this is how I approach the matter.

I say to myself, if it doesn't feel old and it doesn't look old then I must be very sceptical about its genuineness. Call me whatever you will but I think that if an object has survived a couple of centuries then it must necessarily be different in some way than an object which has just jumped off the factory floor. Too clean and shiny makes me suspicious; too sparkling paintwork makes me suspicious; and too crisp edging makes me suspicious. The marks on bases mean nothing; well, not a lot. Yes, I go by the premise that if I don't think it is old then it isn't old, and sometimes I get it wrong, but I have no regrets.

I must say here that if you have purchased a piece and it has later aroused your suspicions that it may not be as old as you thought, then pass on these thoughts to potential buyers; be honest with your assessment and they can't return to you and say you did not tell them it was modern.

If you handle genuine items regularly the task of identifying fakes does become slightly easier, however, I would always advise you to be very cautious about spending large sums on items that you are not certain about. Some dealers will guarantee an item's authenticity, and these are well worth trading with. But I would suggest that you should be very aware that the item you are looking at could be a fake, especially if it is Chinese.

THE ART OF DEALING, BUYING AND HAGGLING

The selling of an antique for a huge profit can give you a great boost of satisfaction and solidify your confidence in your abilities as a dealer, but as far as fun goes, as far as enjoyment extends, to me there is nothing comparable with the hunt and the haggling involved in the final deal.

At this stage you may believe that selling is the bees' knees of antique dealing, but that is far from the truth; there can be as much success to be gained from the haggle as there can be from the actual sale; indeed, I have sold many items for less than the dealer I bought it from had it up for sale initially – the haggle can be the most powerful tool in your armoury, certainly it is a very close ally of knowledge.

The better you are at reading reactions, slight nuances in speech, meanings of body movements, displays of interest or lack of interest, eye reaction and facial expression, the more success you will have as a haggler. But everything I am about to say will also apply to how the experienced dealer is viewing you, so beware when you meet your match.

Let us return to the hunt. I am treading gently down the centre of the second aisle at an antique fair when the alarm bell sounds in my head or the searchlight has planted its full beam on the potential escapee. I do not speed up, I remain relaxed, vaguely disinterested and sidle gently over to the table housing the glorious piece of Japanese Satsuma. I may not even look at it but handle another item on the table. I inspect the item in my hand, then gently release it, all the while reading clues about the character of the dealer who watches from the other side of the table. 'Morning,' I'll say, 'you've some nice things here.' The dealer will react, and I get to know a little more about him. I cast my eyes broader and point to the Satsuma piece. 'What you got on that?'

He says a price, let us say £180, then he proceeds to tell you what he knows about it, which in the majority of cases will be 'It's from the Meiji period.' I pick it up, examine the piece closely and tell him something about it that he doesn't know. If at this point he does know more, he will come out with it, and if he comes out with it he will know the true value of the piece. Hopefully, to him it is merely a Satsuma bowl or vase that he wishes to sell. I identify the markings on the base and ascertain that the vase is from the Tasho period which was from 1912-1926 after the Meiji period ended. 'It's 20th century,' I say. If he wishes to sell the vase he will tell me there is movement in the price, and he does. I ask him his very best price and he says he could do £120 because I've told him the piece isn't as old as he thought it was. Then maybe I return it to its position on the table. 'It's not what I thought it was,' I grumble.

I then return to the original piece I picked up and say, 'How does £60 grab you?' as my hand points back to the Satsuma. He'll likely be quick to say '£100'. I know I've got him, the Satsuma is mine, but not for £100. I picked up the vase again, tell him that I could stretch to £65, if that' any good.

He tells me that his very bottom line is £90. He is being honest, holding out his palms face upward. My other hand has already divided four twenty pound note in my pocket. The hand swoops and delivers the £80 to the open palm and I say, '£80, and we have a deal.' I'm thrusting my empty hand out for the handshake. The deal is done.

If I return home and sell the piece for his original asking price I have made £100 profit, but the piece has a value of at least £250, which I knew from the outset, but it shows how much profit the haggling can add to the eventual outcome.

I have hundreds of stories like this one. There are many lessons to be had from such a story. The first lesson is that the object must have a value greater than the dealers' table price, and the second lesson is that you raise your bid in smaller mounts than the dealer comes down with his. You go up in fivers or tenners if he comes down in twenty pluses. A third lesson is that you should never show eagerness to buy a particular item. A fourth lesson is the attention you pay to the dealer himself – you must read his behaviour and assess how far you can go with your haggling without him losing interest in you. A fifth lesson is knowing your onions; if you know more about an item than the selling dealer does, if he is anything like a sensible chap, he will bow to your wisdom. And perhaps a sixth lesson is showing the colour of your money – dealers are at the fair to make money and when it has touched their hand they find it difficult to let go.

I suppose this story raises the question of precisely where you start the haggle. I would suggest at a lower point than the price you are prepared to pay for the item. In the above case my intention was to get this piece of Satsuma for £80, but had I opened at £80 that certainly wouldn't have been the case and a mouthful of profit would have been eaten by my inexperience.

Of course, not all haggles have successful outcomes. You must be prepared to walk away rather than pay more than you wish to. You must also bear in mind that the dealer really does have a bottom line because he must obtain his measure of profit, and he is not going to sell you an item and make a loss.

But haggling is tremendous fun and I often receive amusing comments from friendly dealers. They say, 'Go away, and don't come back again,' wearing a huge grin. They'll tell me that 'They've been mugged.' But this is all part of the camaraderie that exists between antique dealers. They know that I am a buyer, and furthermore, they know I will return to buy more of their wares.

It does not mean that 100% of purchases have been the result of haggling. There are extremely rare cases when you find something and it is worth every penny and more. You can be generous, and occasionally give them the money if they have made a drastic underestimation in pricing.

RESEARCHING VALUES AND IDENTIFICATION

You've bought your item, inspected it, cleaned it, and it is ready to go on your selling site. Presumably as you have parted with a chunk of money you already know roughly what the items is and its approximate value, but the guesswork ends here, you needs to be more precise in order to get the maximum amount of profit from your item.

Wouldn't it be wise to know its decade of manufacture, the location where it was created, the person or factory who made it, the name of its pattern if it has a pattern, its width and height, its condition in comparison with similar items, its commonness or rarity, What it is it made of, and its highest and lowest value? Not in all cases can you find out the answer to these questions, but you can do your best in trying to answer them.

There are many internet antique sites which allow you to enter a succinct description of your item and the site will offer many images of similar items for you to inspect. In most cases tracking down something very similar to your purchase is a quick process. Other sellers will have recorded much of the information that you are seeking. If the first sites don't offer similar pieces, then persist until you have found success. Always note values for those pieces that are most like your item, and always bear in mind that some sellers put unrealistic values on things they are selling. The more you research, the more accurate your pricing becomes.

With rarer items it is not always a few minutes or a few hours that will yield a result. However, this is not such a bad outcome because if the internet offers nothing like your prize item then you may be on to a winner. If this happens to you then ask an amount of money you would be happy to accept, and then sit back to see what happens.

I should also warn you about matching values of items which have been listed for sale in the United States. For a reason unbeknown to me it appears often that the Americans think of a high number and attach it to anything resembling an antique; if you use a similar practise I can assure you that few sales in Britain will be forthcoming. I do trade both ways with the USA but trading and pricing are different matters,

If you have identified your item and attached as much detail as possible to its description, and listed it at a price which is reasonable, it will in time sell. There is no rush to dispose of it: the buyer will arrive when he or she meets your item on a computer screen.

AUCTION/BUY IT NOW/BEST OFFER

I have touched briefly on the virtues of EBay and I'm convinced that at least for me, this is the number one selling site for antiques. Not only does it offer a vast market place, having customers throughout the world, but there are three ways to sell an item: by auction, having a fixed price which is buy it now, and a price which is open to best offers.

For the reason I am guiding you to an ever increasing value on your stock of items I must suggest that auctions do not fit in with this idea. However, It is fair to suggest that when you reach a position of being willing to take risks, and perhaps suffer set-backs when items fetch lower prices than those you paid for them isn't a retrograde step, you may dabble with the notion of the auction, but until this happens I recommend one of the other options.

The buy it now option allows you to dictate the absolute price. If you put your item up for sale you will get the stated amount when you sell. But let's be reasonable here and imagine that car boot sales and antique fairs worked under this principle; the haggle goes out of the window and you are condoning a take it or leave it trading platform. For me this is too much like going to the supermarket with ten other people and filling your baskets with identical goods. At the checkout we all get charged the same: my skill as a buyer is no better or worse than the ten people who shopped with me. Fixed prices offer no sense of striking a deal, and for this reason I would steer you towards the buy it now price with the best offer option.

When your goods are listed under the buy it now/best offer option customers are free to make offers, which can be accepted, rejected, or met with a counter offer. You have the choice to make a deal or refuse the deal, just as you do when haggling at the antiques fair. It seems to me a very good system whereby you can assess your potential profit before responding to the bid.

Naturally with the best offer option you get occasional chancers offering pitiful amounts for valuable items. You simply press the decline offer button which either sends them packing or they can return with a more sensible offer.

LISTINGS (FEES, PHOTOGRAPHS, ACCURACY & HONESTY)

Listing items on EBay is a straightforward affair. When you have listed many items, then the time for each item is probably less than two minutes, and I believe that on a smartphone the process is even quicker. Your items will appear on your pages together with their headings and the prices you are asking, and of course there will be a purchase button for customers. It is simply a case of waiting for sales to come.

The listing should contain several sharp photographs with nothing but the item in the frame, and preferably against a single colour background; white being the best. Your photographs should cover every angle of the item, including a picture of the base and any identifications marks. All imperfections should be detailed in order for the customers to see clearly what they are buying.

The title should give as much information as the title line provides for, and other information such as dimensions and a condition report should appear in the description paragraph.

Be accurate in everything you write, and if you are uncertain about any particular aspect, then either don't say it or express your uncertainty in words. Just be honest, for honesty is preferable to deceit. A potential buyer desires to read a few words from a genuine seller and not read a stream of garbage from a fraud.

Take a look at the antiques offered on EBay and you will quickly notice what differences there are in the expertise and presentation of sellers. You are much more likely to be attracted to good presentation than a dark photograph and a short phrase which simply reads 'Grandma's old bowl.'

As for fees, they are considerably cheaper than expenses incurred by attending and setting up at antique fairs. EBay does take commission, and there are nominal listing fees, and off course Paypal has small fees too, but largely you are dealing with fees that for the majority are paid out of your profits. Fees are as much to worry about as the petrol you put in your car to continue buying and my advice is not to give fees a thought; if you are paying fees you are succeeding, and if you are paying lots of fees you are having enormous success.

PACKAGING AND POSTING

I'll deal with packaging first and you must believe that what I tell you is true. The postal system is brutal, in some countries more brutal that others. Superman in a box would not survive the Chinese postal service unless he was wrapped in many layers of padding, and you must believe this is vaguely true about other postal systems.

Wrap your items so they are extremely well protected, and porcelain very well protected indeed, or you will receive a message from your buyer stating that the item has arrived broken. Never place anything in a box without padding. Never allow anything to be loose inside a box. The box should be filled so no vacant spaces exist within it.

It is a good practice to ship items as soon as possible after the sale, certainly within 24 hours. Many sellers don't do this, but you are trying to establish a good reputation, for both efficiency and honesty, and by being prompt with your dispatches; customers will soon commend you for your service.

Postage itself is paid by the buyer, but if you wish to offer free postage then you should factor this expense into your selling price.

AGAIN RAISING THE STAKES

If you recall the first line of the plan began with 1+1+1+1+1+1+1+1+1+1=10, suggesting that you took your single stake and bought ten items of similar value, and then await your sales in order to progress to further lines of the plan. I'm sure you will have questioned the limited purchases idea and thought that you were capable of making greater investment – well, congratulations to you. The whole purpose was to get you started and to get you believing that you can do better than the plan suggests. No doubt that after several months of trading your antiques stockroom is filling up nicely, and you have already stopped purchasing those basic items which held some attraction in the first few weeks. The value of your stock already will be exceeding your expectations and you will be looking forward to the future knowing the best is yet to come.

So keep raising your stakes. On each visit to the places where you buy keep on looking for better and better things that will attract new customers with plenty of money to spend. Keep on learning about areas you have not covered, and also learn more about the more valuable items in areas you know something about.

It is not necessary to increase the number of items in your stock to a degree where your house is beginning to look like a shop. When you are achieving your goals easily, look to buy increasing numbers of quality items, and as I've said before, do not seek to replace the cheap things even if they are available: I am aware that all items attract customers but you must say to yourself that you are heading to the premiership rather than remaining in the lower divisions.

The growth of stock value can be rapid with constant reinvestment and a determination to search for quality. I remember when I made a concerted effort to step up a few gears, and in no time at all increased the value of my stock from £2,000 to £20,000. It simply takes a frame of mind which tells you that the progress can be done quickly. However, all progress necessarily must be linked to learning, and the learning should not be slapdash or shallow: the greater your depth of knowledge, the more certainty you have when making a purchase and that this is the correct purchase that ensures profit.

Very soon you convince yourself that the beginning is way behind you. A single purchase of say £80 may result in a sale around £300, and you think back at all the items you bought at the outset and realise that one sale has put the multitude to shame.

Each month that passes gives you increasing confidence. You are able to dream of where you are going and where this business has the potential to take you. Already you will know the truth of the statement that knowledge is power, and you will know too that this is a game, and he who knows most wins.

ALTERING PRICES

Perhaps a brief word should be said about tampering with your prices. I do not do this often but there have been occasions when I've overvalued an item and it has received little or no interest. If you find this happens to you, then every month of two, decrease the price of these items slightly until interest is gained.

I am from time to time also minded to get rid of cheap items gathering dust. Of course a buyer will come along eventually but if you find that you're short of storage space, then reduce these prices too and get rid of your clutter; these small reductions will hardly affect your total stock value.

Generally, the asking prices you initially choose will be fine for months. The customers who do find merit in your offerings will always have the best offer button to press and they can submit bids if interested.

BECOMING AN EXPERT AND CONFIDENCE

At the start of each season take yourself back to the day when you wondered about buying such a book as this. You probably had a mild curiosity for antiques but thought the business would be complicated, too much hard work to get involved in. If you are like me you maybe thought too you'd never be able to recognise all those millions of different wares and what use would it be with only sufficient knowledge to identify things you already knew about.

Take yourself back too to the day you took your first tentative steps along the aisles of antiques when the dealers wares were mysteries and carried price tags which you deemed unaffordable, or at least excessive. Maybe, again as I did, you thought what am I do here and there is no possibility that I will ever feel at home here, let alone enjoy the banter of haggling.

Once you knew nothing. Once it was all so strange.

Expertise doesn't drop from the sky and dress you in the garb of an antique dealer but it comes from steadily collecting knowledge as slowly and as carefully the mountaineer's steps as he climbs the mountain. Throughout the experience of going from complete novice to buyer extraordinaire it is merely a belief that the plan is flawless which fuels you, and if you desire riches, then they are accessible and the plan will take you there. There is no difference between setting off to walk to Australia to setting off to make your fortune; in both cases you will fail if you turn back, and in both cases you will succeed if you remain on course.

Expertise in anything necessitates the continual collecting of knowledge and a constant realisation that there is still so much to know. But collecting gets easier and easier because you have so much previously collected knowledge to which new knowledge can be attached.

And as you feel your expertise growing, so too the confidence in your abilities soars beyond whatever you formerly imagined. You will view items for sale with knowledge where once you asked yourself question and once stood at an antiques table with hesitancy in your veins. You will know that the power is with you and the decision of whether to buy or not to buy is an easy decision, one made solely on the items' profitability. At every step you will never hesitate, you will never consider that it can't be taken. The tens of thousands of steps you have already taken allow you the privilege of knowing you are an antique dealer – a successful antique dealer at that.

BECOMING MASTER OF YOUR FUTURE

As I told you quite early in this book the reason I set off on this trail was to show my adult children that wealth is attainable if your desire for wealth is strong, and if you stick to a flawless plan that will deliver wealth. Whether any of them decide to pursue such an idea is up to them, but for myself I'll probably continue with antiques for a few more years before I accept that it is taking up too much of the time that I could devote to writing more books.

But in a few short years you will be in a position to become master of your destiny. You may decide that millionairehood is for you and the desire to mix with those in the Sotheby's and Christies' auction houses is strong. There is no limit to what you can achieve or to what heights you can climb in this business. It all depends on knowing more than those around you, it all depends on how much progress you are prepared to make and how much wealth you desire to accumulate.

I have not a shred of doubt that to progress from £20,000 worth of stock to £100,000 worth of stock is easy. From £100,000 to £1,000,000 would be easier still providing that you keep on learning and meeting every challenge in your path.

At any point, if you become satisfied and wish to sell all your items then the auction house will gladly accommodate you.

Up to now I have never once referred to income that may have found its way into your pocket. Probably you are surprised that excess money has come your way. Even though you constantly reinvest, the potential for income increase from day one. Even well before line 10 of the plan you are finding you have more cash than you had prior to starting this enterprise. The good news is that you will have more and more cash even after your reinvestments have been made.

The future is yours to direct however you see fit. You are empowered to become master of your destiny.

A FAVOUR IN RETURN

There will be readers who will get to the end of this book whose hopes and dreams will forever remain hopes and dreams, and I wish you all the best and thank you for taking time out to read my work

There will also be those of you who say to yourself, 'I want some of that,' and you will progress through the lines of the plan and hopefully make yourselves a small fortune. You could possibly become super rich.

But my request for favour is this, reserved for the time you have earned your first few thousand pounds, which won't be long in coming. I ask you to purchase from Amazon Books UK my last novel A CROSS OF CROCUSES by Ken Ross. It is quite a sad tale loosely based on the last couple of years of my parents' lives. It is a story which older people will empathise with and make them think about both their loved ones and their destiny in a completely different way.

For me, purchase a copy and give it to an older relation. They will come back to thank you and tell you that they've read a story like none they've read before. And when you've reached a £100,000 please buy ten more copies and give them away. I am not needy of the royalties, but it is my duty to keep the memory of my mother and my father alive.   Thank you.

Printed in Great Britain
by Amazon